BOB GELDOF

Other titles in the
PEOPLE WHO MADE A DIFFERENCE
series include

Marie Curie
Father Damien
Mahatma Gandhi
Martin Luther King, Jr.
Mother Teresa

North American edition first published in 1990 by
Gareth Stevens Children's Books
1555 North RiverCenter Drive, Suite 201
Milwaukee, Wisconsin 53212, USA

First published in the United Kingdom in 1989. This edition
is abridged from the original published in 1988 by Exley
Publications Ltd. and written by Charlotte Gray. Copyright
© 1987 by Exley Publications. Additional end matter © 1990
by Gareth Stevens, Inc.

For a free color catalog describing
Gareth Stevens' list of high-quality
children's books, call

**1-800-341-3569 (USA) or
1-800-461-9120 (Canada)**

Library of Congress Cataloging-in-Publication Data

Adrian-Vallance, D'Arcy.
    Bob Geldof : champion of Africa's hungry people / by Charlotte
Gray ; this edition written by D'Arcy Adrian-Vallance. — North
American ed.
        p.   cm. — (People who made a difference)
    ISBN 0-8368-0391-4
    1. Geldof, Bob, 1954- —Juvenile literature. 2. Live Aid (Fund
raising enterprise) 3. Rock musicians—Ireland—Biography—
Juvenile literature. I. Gray, Charlotte, 1927-   Bob Geldof. II.
Title. III. Series.
ML3930.G27A66   1990   782.42166'092—dc20a
[B]   89-77588

PICTURE CREDITS
Associated Press — 39 (below), 40, 42,
43, 44 (below left), 45 (left); © David
Bailey (from *Imagine, a book for Band Aid*)
— 27 (top); Express Newspapers plc —
28; Lafayette, Dublin — 4, 6, 8; London
Features International Ltd. — Steve
Rapport 38, 39 (top): Ken Regan
(Camera 5) 48-49; Marconi Space
Systems — 33; © Tony McGrath — 19;
Monitor Press — 15; Duncan Paul
Associates — Brian Aris 34; the Press
Association — 23, 54, 58; Tom Redman
— cover illustration; Retna Pictures Ltd.
— Adrian Boot 13, 41, 44 (below right),
45 (right), 60-61: Larry Busacca 44 (top):
Paul Slattery 17; *Sunday Times*, London,
from *With Geldof in Africa* — Frank
Herrmann, 21, 24, 27 (below), 29, 52-53,
56, 57; Times Books Ltd., from *With
Geldof in Africa* — 25; Universal Pictorial
Press & Agency Ltd. — 36-37.
    Map on page 11 drawn by
Geoffrey Pleasance.

Our grateful thanks to the many
agencies and photographers for
their help and especially to David
Bailey, Tony McGrath, and Times
Books Ltd. for donating their fees
directly to Band Aid.

Series conceived and edited by Helen Exley
Series editors, U.S.: Amy Bauman and Rhoda Irene Sherwood
Additional end matter, U.S.: Meredith Ackley
Research editor, U.S.: John D. Rateliff
Cover design: Kate Kriege

Printed in Hungary

1 2 3 4 5 6 7 8 9 96 95 94 93 92 91 90

*Champion
of Africa's
hungry people*

BOB
GELDOF

**D'Arcy
Adrian-Vallance's
adaptation of
the book by
Charlotte Gray**

Gareth Stevens Children's Books
MILWAUKEE

Early days

Robert (Bob) Frederick Zenon Geldof was born in Ireland in 1954, on the outskirts of Dublin. His father's parents had come from Belgium in 1914 to escape from the First World War. His mother's parents were German. His unusual middle name, Zenon, was chosen by his father. Geldof said on television, "My father wanted to call me Zeus Zenon, but my mother wouldn't wear it."

Geldof had two sisters, Cleo and Lynn. They were older than he. The family was strong and loving and had plenty of good times. As a young boy, Bob Geldof was bright, cheerful, and always on the go.

Just before Bob started school, the family moved to a new house. The new house was in Dun Laoghaire, outside Dublin. It was big and gloomy, but Geldof's father made it bright with new paint. But then his mother died, and everything changed. She died so suddenly that seven-year-old Bob could hardly understand what had happened.

About five years later, Geldof's sister Cleo became very ill. Everyone expected that she would die too, but she did not. Soon after Cleo was well again, she got married and moved away. His sister

Opposite: Bob Geldof at school at Blackrock College, Dublin. Many years later, this boy became a famous pop star. To help the poor, he put together the world's biggest concert. Through the concert, he raised more money for Africa's poor people than any other person in the world.

On some days, school was like prison. Then Bob would get away at lunchtime to sit on the sea wall. From here, he used to stare out to sea.

Lynn had also left. So that meant Bob was the only child living in the big house.

At the time, Geldof went to an expensive private school called Blackrock College. Some of the children came to school only during the day. Others were boarders who lived at the school. Because his father was gone all day, Bob stayed at school until late evening. He ate supper there and stayed through the evening study time. The students who lived at Blackrock College were unkind to Geldof. He had to sit at a separate table, and they often made fun of him because he was a day student.

However, there was one thing about the evenings that Bob enjoyed. Sometimes, students were asked to sing, act, or play music before supper. The other pupils hated this, but Bob loved it.

Geldof's teenage years were difficult. He hated school. He was intelligent but never did well. He did not care about his appearance. Geldof's father worried that his son looked so scruffy and seemed interested only in rock groups such as the Rolling Stones and the Who. To the younger Geldof, it seemed that his father was always angry with him.

But at fourteen, Bob Geldof was no different from other people his age. He wanted a life of his own. He wanted to shake up his teachers and the other adults around him. He thought their ideas were boring and old-fashioned.

There was one thing that helped Bob through this difficult time of his life. It was his music — the music that his father and teachers didn't understand. The songs of the Rolling Stones meant a lot to him. Mick Jagger's words made him feel less awkward and strange.

His father taught him a lot, too. Many years later, Geldof's sister Cleo spoke to London's *Today* newspaper. She said, "I think we learned a good deal from Daddy. He always kept our minds working, made us aware of the world, taught us to question. But more than that, he's a very kind man, always quietly helping people in trouble."

Geldof has helped people, too — millions of people. He is still angry, and some people say he can be rude. But he

Blackrock College, a private school, stands just outside Dublin. Geldof was never happy there.

believes that it is better to be rude and say what is on his mind than to be polite and tell lies. He still looks as messy as he did at school. But people accept it now. Important people, such as the heads of countries, are pleased to meet him and listen to his words.

Geldof's last years at school were awful. He was always in trouble, and the teachers never seemed pleased with him. But it was also in his final year at school that he began working with the Simon Communities in Dublin. The Simon Communities were set up to help poor people, homeless people, and people with drinking or drug problems. The communities give food, clothing, and a bed for the night to anyone who needs it.

Geldof began to see life through the eyes of these poor people. He began to understand their problems and needs.

Later this experience helped him understand the needs of the hungry people in Africa.

Geldof worked two nights a week at the Simon Community. He often did not get to bed until 5:00 A.M. Then he still had to go to school. He began to feel that his work at the Simon Community was the real part of his life. It was there he learned about life.

At last, it was time for final exams. Geldof sat at a desk in a large room. His test papers were in front of him: a paper listing questions and a paper for answers. He wrote his name at the top of the answer paper. Then he put his pen down and thought about other things until the test period was over.

The last day of school finally came. Freedom at last. His father wanted him to stay, but Bob had had enough. He left Ireland and went to England.

FREE — more or less

Geldof found that being free was not so easy. He had to have money to live. So he got a job in a factory where peas were put into cans. It was an awful job. The peas smelled horrible. They turned the skin on his hands and arms green. Nothing he did seemed to wash away the smell or the green color.

Bob returned to Ireland. There, he tried one job after another. None seemed right. Before long, he left for Britain again. This time, he got a job as part of a road construction crew. For a while, he had a good time with the other crew members. But in the end, Geldof decided that it was not the right job for him either.

He went to London. There he found an empty house and began living in it with some other young people. For a few months, he moved from house to house and from job to job. It was a bad time for him. He started taking drugs and became ill. From this experience, he learned the dangers of drugs. He now tells people not to use them.

Geldof had a friend named Shaun Finnigan. Shaun told him about a job at a language school in Spain. Bob was ready to get away from London. He wanted to get his health back. So he went to Spain with Shaun. But after only a year in Spain, the school closed.

Bob was soon back in Dublin again. The city seemed to close around him like a prison. Bob began to make new plans. This time, he went to Canada.

Reporter in Canada

Geldof arrived in Canada with very little money. In Vancouver, he passed himself off as a reporter. He had never had training or experience as a writer. But he found he could write well — and he enjoyed it. He wrote well enough to

EIRE AND THE UNITED KINGDOM OF GREAT BRITAIN

Dublin

Dun Laoghaire

SCOTLAND

NORTHERN IRELAND

Liverpool

Lincoln

EIRE

ENGLAND

WALES

Cardiff

London

Davington

become music editor for the *Georgia Straight*. He did the job well and found he could make decent money writing.

Being a music editor was a more important job than being a reporter of straight news. As editor, Geldof had to write about pop music across the vast country of Canada. His writing brought him success. People all over the country began to value his opinion. They also wanted his friendship.

Bob Geldof is Irish. He was born in Dublin, the capital of Ireland (or Eire). The Geldof family later moved to Dun Laoghaire. Today, Geldof lives in London. He also has a second home in Davington, Kent, England.

For the first time in his life, Bob Geldof felt that people were looking up to him. They were interested in what he said and wrote. Geldof felt alive and strong at last. He was full of new ideas and plans. He wanted to stay in Canada forever.

By this time, Geldof had been in Canada for three years. But to become a Canadian citizen, he needed documents. This meant going back to Ireland. So, in 1975, he left for Ireland to get the papers.

Back in Dublin, he had to wait a long time. Soon, he was bored. So he decided to start a free newspaper. He had seen free newspapers in Vancouver, but Dublin had none. Starting a new business would not be easy, but Geldof thought he would give it a try.

Getting nowhere

At the same time, some of Bob's old friends had started a rock group. The group's members were Pete Briquette, Gerry Cott, Simon Crowe, Johnnie Fingers, and Gary Roberts. None of them had played in other bands. None of them was famous.

Gary, who played rhythm guitar, suggested that Bob should be the group's manager. Instead, Bob became the lead singer of the group. He was very serious about the band. He wanted it to be new and different from other bands. Most of all, he wanted it to be successful.

Then, one day in September 1975, Gerry brought them some news. He had found some work for the band. They were going to play at a dance hall on October 30. They would get about $60 — the band's first paid work. The date was only a month away. Bob was afraid that they could never be ready in time. It would be a disaster, he thought. The band must get out of it.

So Geldof told the promoter that the group wouldn't play for $60. He said they wouldn't play for less than $120. He was certain that the promoter would not pay them that much. But he was wrong.

Bob, Johnnie, Pete, Gerry, Gary, and Simon were the Boomtown Rats. They were one of the 1970s' punk rock bands. Their first number-one song was "Rat Trap."

13

The promoter agreed to pay the fee that Bob had set. Now the band had to play.

The Boomtown Rats

October 30 came. The band members were nervous when they arrived at the dance hall. They did not feel ready. They did not even have a name for the band. They came up with "Nightlife Thugs."

Soon they were standing on a stage in front of everyone. They began to play. People started to dance. The group could not believe it. People were enjoying their music! They played another song, and the dancers loved it. Geldof and his friends felt great. They were a real band.

During a break, Geldof remembered a book about a teenage gang in a boom town in the United States. From that, he came up with a better name for the group. He erased "Nightlife Thugs" from the blackboard where it was written and wrote "The Boomtown Rats."

After that, Geldof wanted everyone to know the Boomtown Rats. If the band was going to be successful, they had to get their name in the newspapers. Bob knew how to do this because he had worked for the press. Soon newspapers began to write about the Boomtown Rats. The number of fans grew.

The Boomtown Rats were successful because their music was different. And they and their music could make people

enjoy themselves. Geldof had some unusual ideas that helped, too. For example, one night the group gave a piece of raw meat to the best dancer! It was a strange idea, but it made people remember the group. Sometimes, there was trouble with the police at concerts. That made them even more famous. Their concerts were always sold out.

Life was good for Geldof. But the group was still not making enough money to live on. Although he was becoming famous, Bob was still delivering bread three days a week. All the same, things were moving fast.

The band went on tour, playing in different parts of Ireland. The tour ended at Dublin National Stadium. There was not an empty seat. But even after the tour, the Boomtown Rats were still not rich. The tour cost almost as much as they had earned.

In April 1977, the group went to England. They played in clubs around the country. The record companies soon heard about them. They liked what they heard, and six companies asked the band to make a record for them. The Boomtown Rats chose one of the companies, Ensign Records, and got ready to make their first record.

The Boomtown Rats were like many other "new wave" bands of the 1970s. But they were different, too. Bob believed that audiences wanted not only to hear music but also to see a good show. They wanted to be part of it. So Geldof talked to the band's audiences, and he won them over every time.

Fame and success

Suddenly, the Boomtown Rats were more successful than they had ever expected to be. In 1977, they moved to Britain. They made their first hit single, "Looking After Number One." Their first album, *The Boomtown Rats*, was a hit too. They toured northern England and did a television show in Ireland. Later, they were on a national television show in Britain, "Top of the Pops." In 1978, their single "Rat Trap" became the number-one record in Britain.

In 1977, Paula Yates had come into Geldof's life. Bob did not want to have only one girlfriend, but Paula had already decided what she wanted. When the band moved, Paula moved. In the end, Bob found that he was in love. They have been together ever since.

In 1979, the Boomtown Rats were Britain's top band. The single "I Don't Like Mondays" went to number one and stayed there for weeks. Geldof was working very hard writing songs, making videos, talking to reporters, working on new ideas, and performing every night in front of big audiences.

Paula Yates behind Bob. She was seventeen when they met. Nine years later, they were married.

Geldof liked fame; it gave him a chance to speak his mind. Sometimes people were shocked by his opinions and his strong language. But success can come and go. Show business is hard. The public can love a band one day and forget them the next day.

After four years of success, things began to go badly for the Boomtown Rats. They were making records, but the records were not big hits. Geldof was worried. In June 1982, he and Paula had a baby daughter, Fifi Trixiebelle. It was the worst time to have money worries.

The band went on working hard for two years. Their sixth album, *In the Long Grass*, was made in 1984. Critics said it was good, but few people bought it.

One evening in October 1984, Bob felt very low. He came home, sat down, and turned on the television. What he saw on the television made his troubles seem small. What he saw changed his life and the lives of millions of people.

That night, Bob Geldof saw pictures of the terrible famine in Ethiopia. He saw people who had not eaten for weeks. They were thin, weak, and had lost all hope. One mother held her dying child. The child was too weak to cry or to ask for help. Other people were counting the children that were already dead. The television reporter was so shocked that he could hardly speak. And the reporter

was also angry that this terrible thing was happening. He wanted to know who had let it happen.

If this had happened to a few families, it would be terrible enough. But here, tens of thousands of people were starving to death in front of the cameras. Some aid workers were there, but they had only enough food for a few people. The workers had to choose who to feed and who to let die.

In October 1984, pictures of the famine in Ethiopia were first shown on television all over the world. The United Nations called it "the greatest natural disaster."

A record by the stars
Bob Geldof and millions of other people were shocked that night. In their

Opposite: After Geldof had seen starving children like this, he wasn't afraid to ask people for help. He would push and push until they agreed to help. He said later, "Maybe I was given my arrogance for this." The prize was Britain's best-selling record of all time and millions of dollars that would save people from death.

comfortable living rooms, with food and drink only steps away, they stared at their television sets.

Geldof could not sleep that night. He had completely forgotten his own money worries. But the pictures from the television stayed in his head. What could he do? Send money, yes. But what else? He was not an important person, and he was not rich. He was a pop musician. What could a pop musician do?

He could make a record. If people bought the record, he could send the money to Ethiopia. But the Boomtown Rats were going through a bad time. People might not buy the record.

Then Geldof had an idea. If the Boomtown Rats couldn't make a successful record, maybe some other top stars could.

Midge Ure of Ultravox was a good friend. Geldof phoned him, and Midge agreed to help. He even came up with a name for their campaign to raise money through rock bands: "Band Aid."

What about Sting? He was very successful. Geldof phoned him and explained that he wanted to make a record before Christmas to raise money for Ethiopia. Could Sting help?

Yes. "I'll be there," Sting said.

Midge Ure and Sting were famous names. They were very busy people. But they were glad to help.

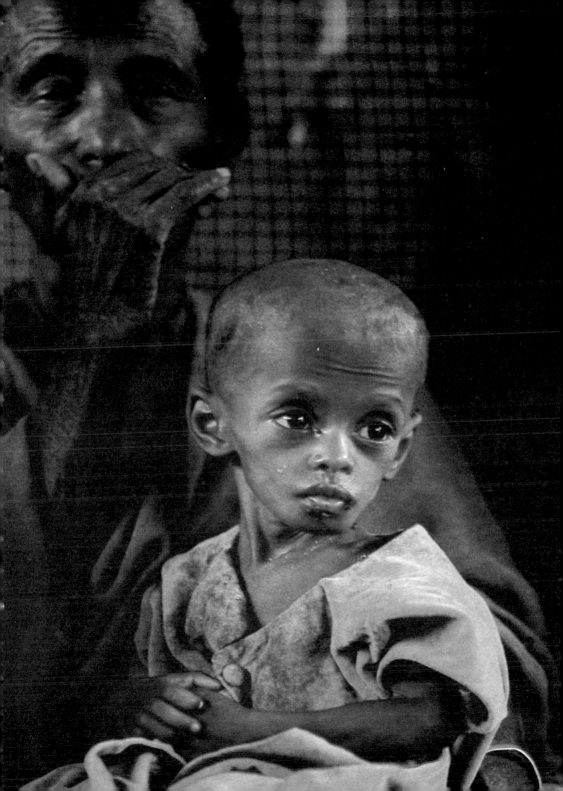

Next, Geldof phoned Simon le Bon of Duran Duran. Yes, Duran Duran would be able to help out, too. He then met with Gary Kemp of Spandau Ballet. The group was going to Japan for a two-week tour. They would sing with the others if Geldof could delay the recording.

That was the problem. These musicians were very busy people. They traveled a lot. They had all arranged tours, concerts, and recordings months before. How could they all get together on one day at one recording studio in London before Christmas?

Geldof phoned more musicians: Boy George, Frankie Goes to Hollywood, Style Council. Midge Ure helped with the song they would sing, but Geldof wrote the words in the back of a taxi. . . . "Do They Know It's Christmas?"

A lot of people helped. The record company said Geldof would not have to pay for the studio. Everybody in the company agreed to work without pay.

It could be big

David Bowie and Paul McCartney could not come but would send recordings. The artwork was ready. The artists had done the record cover without pay. The art was excellent. A recording date was chosen — Sunday, November 25, 1984.

Geldof asked the newspapers to write about the record on their front pages.

"Is the record boring? 'Who cares?' says Geldof. It could have consisted of people yawning — the point was to buy it. Is it an exaggeration to compare, as Geldof did, the African famine to the Nazi Holocaust? Not so, he claims. More people may die in Africa, and more people could — but won't — save their lives."
Michael Elliott,
in Cosmopolitan,
June 1985

One newspaper said "No, maybe page two." Geldof was very angry. He phoned the owner of the newspaper. He told the owner that millions of people were starving to death. This record could help them. How could he say no?

The newspaper owner agreed to report the record on the front page. Geldof had learned a lesson: Always go straight to the top.

Meanwhile, more stars had agreed to sing on the Band Aid record. Geldof was working all day and all night. There were so many things to organize, and he was at the center of it all.

The day for the recording came. Geldof half wondered if anybody would come. At the studio, the stars began to arrive. All the stars of British pop. All except Boy George. He was still in America when Geldof phoned him. He caught the next Concorde flight and arrived in time to sing.

They finished making "Do They Know It's Christmas?" at 7:00 A.M. the next morning. Immediately, Geldof took the record to the British Broadcasting Corporation (BBC) and asked them to play it. The BBC let him speak on the radio. He told the listeners about Band Aid and the record. He told everyone to buy the record for their friends and families at Christmas. He said that every record bought would save lives.

Bob Geldof and Midge Ure receive the Ivor Novello Award for writing the Band Aid record "Do They Know It's Christmas?"

Geldof then asked the BBC to put the song on "Top of the Pops." They did. Britain's number-one song that week was by Jim Diamond. It was Jim's first hit record. That week, in an interview, he told people, "Don't buy my record. Buy Band Aid's record."

The record company was making 320,000 copies of the record every day. But even this amount could not keep up with the demand. The record was selling quickly in the United States, too. In two

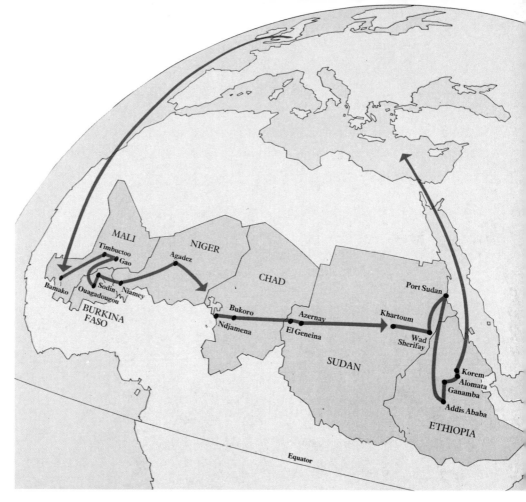

weeks, 1.5 million copies were sold. Soon, it had raised more than $5.7 million to help starving people in Africa.

The newspapers said that Geldof had to go to Africa. He did not want to go. It seemed too big a job; but he went. On January 6, 1985, he flew to Addis Ababa, the capital of Ethiopia.

In October 1985, Bob Geldof traveled to the six African countries where the famine was the worst. He studied the problems of the countries, and spoke to government officials, aid workers, and hungry people.

Ethiopia

When Geldof arrived in Ethiopia, he learned fast. The refugee camps were not a real answer to the problem of famine, but they were keeping people alive. The camps were even worse than they seemed in those terrible pictures he had seen on television. The cameras could not show the heat, the insects, the smell, or the disease.

He saw a child who was about two years old — the same age as his own daughter. The child was as small as a baby. His eyes were full of dirt and insects. He had no clothes. He had eaten dry grain, and it had torn his insides. There was no hope for him.

Geldof went to see important people. He met political officials from the Ethiopian government and other foreign governments. He met aid officials from the European and American relief agencies. Officials have to be very polite. They have to choose their words very carefully. Bob Geldof did not.

One important official began a polite, careful speech. Geldof told him to stop. He told the official to be honest. "Tell me what is needed and how your government can help." The man tried not to answer. But Bob Geldof is good at making people answer. He hit the table with his hand and made the man answer.

While there, Geldof met one very special woman. This little old woman in worn-out shoes knew all about famine, death, and disease. She was Mother

Above, opposite: While this child and millions of other children were dying in Africa, Europe had two million tons of food that it did not need. Early in 1985, Europe threw away all that extra food. It cost over $300 million just to throw it away.

Below, opposite: In Africa, Geldof listened and learned. He wanted to understand the country's problems. He also wanted the Band Aid money to be really useful.

26

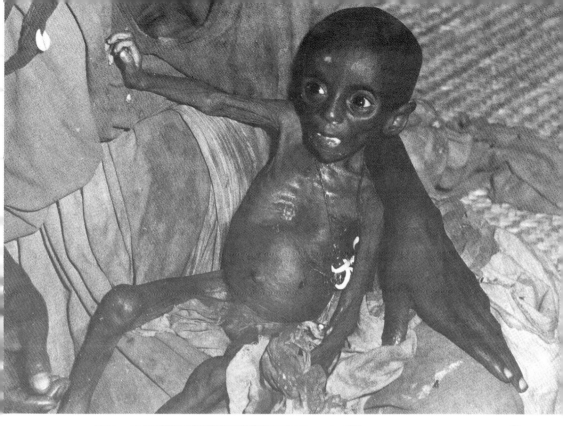

27

Opposite: Geldof takes a
break on his trip through
Africa. There were
always crowds with
him, and he didn't
always enjoy that.

"I can't do what you
can do, and you can't
do what I can do.
But we both have to
do it."

Mother Teresa
to Bob Geldof

Teresa of Calcutta. She was good at
making officials help, too. In front of the
television cameras, she asked one
Ethiopian official for help. She wanted to
use two old palaces as orphanages.

The official said, "I'm sure we can find
you suitable premises for an orphanage."

"Two orphanages," she said.

"Two orphanages," he agreed weakly.

From Ethiopia, Geldof flew to Sudan.
In Sudan, the officials told him that
everything was under control. Tens of
thousands of people were dying. The
camps had no food, water, or toilets. Yet
the officials said all was under control.

At one camp in Sudan there were no houses or tents. There were only two doctors for twenty-seven thousand people. The camp store had only fifteen bags of food. Geldof could see that millions of people would soon starve in Sudan. But the Band Aid money was for Ethiopia. More money was needed.

Back in London, Geldof tried to go back to his work as a Boomtown Rat. But everyone wanted him to give speeches and to talk on television.

In the United States, American rock stars were making an aid record of their own. They asked Geldof to sing on the record, too. So he flew to the United States to record "We Are the World." It all seemed a long way from his school days at Blackrock College.

The stars were working hard in the studio: Bob Dylan, Diana Ross, Michael Jackson, Paul Simon, Dionne Warwick, Stevie Wonder, Tina Turner, Ray Charles, Bruce Springsteen. . . . They all worked without pay, just as the musicians in London had. Soon, other countries were making records for Africa, too.

An idea began to grow in Geldof's head. British and American stars were making records together. . . . Why not have a live concert? It would be a big concert . . . the biggest ever. Britain, America — the whole world — would work together for Africa. Live Aid!

The idea is born

After the USA (United Support of Artists) for Africa recording, Bob Geldof made a speech. He told the American stars about his idea for a concert. The British Band Aid record had raised over $9 million. But it was not enough. Twenty-two million people were starving. The money would keep them alive for only two weeks. They had to raise more money. Geldof asked the stars to help him.

His idea began to take shape. It would not be just one concert in one place. There would be a British concert, an American concert, and concerts all over the world and all at the same time. An international television link would bring them all together. It would be one big concert — a world concert — and the whole world would watch.

Geldof began to make notes. He talked to friends about his ideas. "Great!" they said. But many people didn't think it was possible. It would be too big and too difficult to organize.

How would you begin? Think about it. You must telephone bands all over the world. A lot of bands are traveling. Their managers often want money in advance. How could they all agree on a concert date? You must reserve big stadiums in America, Britain, Germany, Holland, France, and Japan. You must organize

"While the public school intellectuals were debating the finer points of global politics and the problems that lay ahead when the charity ran out, Geldof was on the phone twenty hours a day organizing how best and how quickest the next life could be saved."
    Barry McIlheney,
    Melody Maker,
    December 27, 1985

31

food, radio, television, advertisements, newspaper reporters, and hundreds of other things. (And you have no money!) Where would you start?

Live Aid — getting ready

Geldof telephoned Wembley Stadium, London's largest. The secretary sounded hopeful. That was enough for Bob. He asked Harvey Goldsmith, the promoter, to help. A promoter's job is to organize concerts and advertisements for them.

Then Geldof started phoning all the most famous bands in the world. The calls to Australia, America, Spain, Canada, Japan, and Italy were expensive. Nearly all of the bands wanted to be involved. They were ready to cancel other concerts. They would fly back from any country in the world. And no one wanted money.

Geldof asked the BBC's Channel 4 for seventeen hours of nonstop television time. The television people said it was impossible. They could not change a whole day's programs. It would cost them over a million dollars.

He then phoned the United States. He asked American promoter Bill Graham to organize the American concert. Graham was pleased to help but very worried. So many things could go wrong.

The list of bands was growing. That was good. But London's Wembley

Stadium would cost about $200 thousand for the day. (It usually cost over a million dollars.) The price was still too high for Geldof. On top of this, he was having trouble finding an American stadium.

The date for the concert was getting close. Geldof was very nervous. He seemed to be in ten places at the same time; he had to be. People were working day and night for the concert's success.

Geldof phoned the airlines. They agreed to carry bands free. He next phoned London's commissioner of police and asked for help. Concert organizers usually have to pay for police at a concert. Police protection for the Live Aid concert would cost over $19 thousand. Geldof wanted it for free. The commissioner agreed.

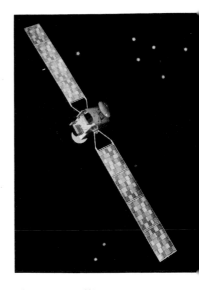

Sixteen satellites sent the Live Aid concert to television sets all over the world.

More problems

Soviet television wanted to show the concert, but there were problems. . . .

The biggest problem was in the United States. Some of the U.S. bands were being difficult. They did not want to cancel their other concert dates for a concert that might not happen. But they worried that people would think badly of them if they didn't play. Bill Graham, the promoter in the United States, told the musicians that this concert was very important. He told them that without the concert, millions of people would die.

Bob, Paula, and their daughter, Fifi Trixiebelle. Paula Yates is well known to British television viewers. While Bob raised money for Africa, Paula earned money for the family.

The list of performers kept growing: Madonna, Joan Baez, Judas Priest. But there were some unpleasant surprises, too. Geldof was sure that the newspaper *Black Voice* — a newspaper for black people — would want to write about the concert. He thought they would support a concert that would help Africa. But they didn't. They felt there should be more black bands playing.

Geldof asked U.S. president Ronald Reagan to send a message on the day of the concert. President Reagan said he would send one if Margaret Thatcher, Britain's prime minister, would send one, too. But Thatcher would not.

On top of this, Danish television decided it would not show the concert. French television decided that "Pop music is not French." And the American Broadcasting Company (ABC) in the United States was asking for impossible things. The Malaysian television people asked if they could keep the money they raised. Geldof agreed. Malaysia was a poor country itself.

Organizing the concert was becoming a nightmare. Geldof flew to Paris, to New York, back to London, to Philadelphia, and to New York again. Then back to London again. He was dizzy, tired, and growing desperate.

But good things were happening, too. The Canadian Broadcasting Corporation (CBC) made a video. The short video showed a small African child. The child was weak and starving, but he was trying bravely to stand up. He tried again and again. This moving video said everything that Geldof wanted to say. He decided to show the video at the concert.

"Almost everyone agrees that Geldof can be loud and obnoxious, has little politeness or tact, that he uses language that isn't fit for a family newspaper, that he rubs people the wrong way, that he has no patience. . . . Yet this man inspires the kind of trust that even the most respected charities can only dream of. People who would normally pass on by any hitchhiker, who looked like Bob does . . . walk up to Geldof with tears in their eyes and stuff wads of money in his hands."
Nathan Aaseng, in his biography, Bob Geldof: The Man Behind Live Aid

The prince and princess of Wales said they would come.

Bruce Springsteen could not play at the American concert in Philadelphia. He wanted to, but he just couldn't make it. Instead, he offered to pay rent for Wembley Stadium in London.

By now, Geldof was worn out. He was traveling too much and sleeping too little. His back hurt. But he didn't have time to slow down. Before he knew it, it was the day before the concert.

Prince Charles and Princess Diana with Bob Geldof at Wembley Stadium. People from 169 countries watched the Live Aid concert on television. Others heard it on radio.

Live Aid — the day

The morning of July 13, 1985, was beautiful. More than 85 percent of the world's television sets would be tuned into Live Aid. Nearly two billion people would be watching the biggest concert the world had ever seen.

The British concert was going to start at midday. The world would watch parts of the British concert and parts of the concerts in other countries. At 5:00 P.M. London time, the American concert would also come onto the television link. When the British concert finished at 10:00 P.M., the American concert would go on for another five hours.

During the concerts, people on television and radio in each country would ask for money for Africa.

The British and American concerts had cost about $4 million to put on. Ticket sales would earn $7 million. Another $7 million would come from television companies. The day was a success before the first song was sung.

But Geldof, the man who had planned and worked so hard for this day, was having terrible back pain. He had stayed awake all night worrying about what could go wrong.

But now, the crowds poured into the arena. They saw Geldof arriving, and they called, "Good luck, Bob!" He began to feel better.

Elton John.

Behind the stage, the performers were getting ready. Everything seemed a terrible mess! Geldof told himself that everyone knew what they were doing. Some of the helpers had not slept for two days. There had just been so much to do.

The stadium was full. Geldof's father, Paula, and Fifi were there. Prince Charles and Princess Diana arrived.

Bob Geldof — bad boy of Blackrock College, construction worker, and singer — sat with Charles and Diana. When the

Above: At the end of the London concert, Paul McCartney and Pete Townshend carried Geldof onto the stage. Everyone sang together. Geldof saw tears running down the faces of those around him. Later, he said, "Sounds corny, doesn't it?... it wasn't."

Left: David Bowie and Paul McCartney at the end of the concert.

The crowd of eighty thousand at London's Wembley Stadium.

crowd saw Geldof there, they cheered loudly. It was more like a big meeting of very good friends than a concert.

The first piece of music, "God Save the Queen," was played at noon. Then with "Rocking All Over the World," the Live Aid concert began.

After months of work, this was it. Nobody had thought it was possible. The big audience rose to the music: Status Quo, Style Council, and then it was the Boomtown Rats. Geldof went up onto the stage. He forgot his back pain and sang "I Don't Like Mondays."

Then he spoke to the crowd. "I think this is the best day of my life," he said. The Boomtown Rats quickly left the stage. The next performer was Adam

Ant. Everyone had the same amount of time on stage. Nobody tried to get one minute of extra television time.

When Geldof left the stage, he had no time to rest. There was still much he had to do. First, he went to the donations office. In the office, there were hundreds of telephones. Weeks before, British Telecom had asked if twenty telephones would be enough. "I want thousands!" Geldof had said.

Donations were pouring in from Ireland, Geldof's own country. But Britain's donations did not amount to much. Britain is so much larger than Ireland. Why were British people not giving money? If the donations did not come in, the concert would be a failure.

Over 100 thousand people came to the concert at John F. Kennedy Stadium in Philadelphia. A total of 1.5 billion people went to concerts all over the world.

Live Aid was very successful. Phone calls came in at the rate of 190 thousand per hour.

The concert itself was going well. Everyone was having a good time. In Australia, INXS was playing.

In Philadelphia, the American concert had started. Joan Baez followed Bernard Watson. The audience was excited there, and donations were coming in fast.

All over the world, pop stars were playing music to help starving people. Elvis Costello, then in the United States, the Hooters. Vienna came on the television with Opus. Next, Nick Kershaw, then the Four Tops. From The Hague, Holland, came B. B. King, Billy Ocean, and Run-DMC. Belgrade, Yugoslavia, brought Yu Rock Mission.

At Wembley, Sade.

In Philadelphia, Rick Springfield.

And then, back to London for Phil Collins. When Phil Collins had finished, he ran to a helicopter. The helicopter flew him to London's Heathrow Airport. He caught a Concorde flight to the United States. He was going to sing in the Live Aid concert on the other side of the Atlantic! The Concorde pilot flew low over Wembley Stadium, and the crowd cheered.

REO Speedwagon, Howard Jones. From Moscow, the band Autograph. Brian Ferry. Crosby, Stills, and Nash — together for the first time in eight years. Udo Lindenberg sang from Germany. The television links were working.

At 5:00 P.M. London time, the American concert in Philadelphia came on the world's televisions.

What about the donations?

Everyone was having a good time. But what about the donations? Was enough money coming in? In Ireland, the donations added up to over $1.3 million. Women were pulling their wedding rings off their fingers. They were giving their jewelry to save the children of Africa.

The British were still a long way behind. Geldof went to the studio and angrily took a microphone. This was not part of the plan. Right now, the plan did not matter; people were dying. He spoke to the millions of listeners. He told them to send money. "If you've sent your money already, go and bang on the house next door — and tell them to send some," he said. It worked. Thousands of British viewers telephoned. The donations were finally coming.

It was a wonderful afternoon. At Wembley, the crowd cheered U2 and Dire Straits. The sun shone on Queen. The Who came on stage then, together again after three years. Elton John and Kiki Dee. The whole world watched Mick Jagger and David Bowie's video of "Dancing in the Streets" flashed on the big screens. Bowie himself came on stage to a thunder of applause.

The Australian Aid for Africa concert. The Australians raised nearly $4 million for Band Aid.

Tina Turner and Mick Jagger.   *Lionel Ritchie.*

Above: Ashford and Simpson with Teddy Pendergrass. Teddy, in the wheelchair, was on stage for the first time since a bad accident. The crowd cheered him, his voice grew stronger, and tears poured down his face.

Left: Madonna.

Opposite, top: Patti LaBelle.

45

America kept up: Bryan Adams, the Beach Boys, Bo Diddley, Madonna, the Pretenders, Santana. And Teddy Pendergrass. Teddy Pendergrass was in a wheelchair. This was his first concert since an accident three years earlier.

At Wembley, Queen's Freddie Mercury and Brian May came on stage again. Then, Paul McCartney. It was like a dream. The Beatles meant so much to Geldof, and here was McCartney singing in a concert that he had organized.

The British concert was coming to an end. The last song was going to be "Do They Know It's Christmas?" All the performers were going to sing together. Suddenly, Geldof realized that they had not practiced the song together. He quickly gave copies of the song to the crowd of famous performers. They gathered together backstage to practice. Suddenly, it went dark. The electricity had gone. They practiced anyway.

Paul McCartney had just begun his song, "Let It Be," when the microphone went dead. The audience did not care. They sang it for him.

A day to remember

By now, Geldof's back hurt so much that he could hardly stand. He lay down, just for a minute. And he went to sleep.

The next thing he knew, someone was shaking him. They carried him onto the stage. There, he stood with McCartney, Bowie, Pete Townshend, and many others. He had always looked up to these people. Now, he stood with them before a huge, cheering audience.

After ten hours of the best pop music, it was a wonderful end. All the performers were on stage together. Tears poured from their eyes as they sang. The British part of the Live Aid concert came to an end. The crowds left. The arena was empty.

The concert ends

On the other side of the Atlantic, Philadelphia was still awake and singing. The Wembley performers went to a nightclub to watch the international Live Aid concert to its end on television.

Geldof arrived at the nightclub in time to see Phil Collins in Philadelphia. Phil Collins had had the strangest day of them all. He had sung on both sides of the Atlantic in the same concert!

Others followed: Duran Duran, Patti LaBelle, Hall and Oates with Eddie Kendricks and David Ruffin, Mick Jagger with Tina Turner, Bob Dylan, Keith Richard, Ron Wood.

And then, at 11:00 P.M. in the United States and 4:00 A.M. in Britain, it really was the end. The concert drew to a close with the American song for Africa, "We Are the World." It had been the best day

"I have been blessed in my life, and I don't take my good fortune for granted. That's what Live Aid is all about."
Patti LaBelle

"We will move a little from the comfort of our lives to understand their hurt."
Joan Baez

in the history of pop music; it had been a special day in the history of the world. Nobody at the concert would forget that day. It had changed the world a little, and they had all been part of it.

The donations come in

Geldof had hoped to raise about $1.5 million from donations on the day of the concert. By the end of the week, about

$42 million had arrived at the Band Aid offices. On December 31, 1985, Geldof had nearly $92 million. The money was still pouring in from all over the world.

But the work was not finished. Someone had to decide how to spend the money. Bob wanted to go back to his life with the Boomtown Rats. But he couldn't go back yet. He had to find experts — people who really understood

The end of the U.S. concert meant the end of the Live Aid concert. For just one day, the world had come together to do something good.

49

Africa's problems. He had to put the money into the hands of these people. He had to be sure that the food, clothes, and medical aid went to the people who needed it. That was not an easy job. It would take weeks of hard work.

After the party

After the Live Aid concerts, people saw Bob Geldof as a hero. He didn't like this. He did not think he was a hero. He had only helped other people to give. Besides, money would not answer all of Africa's problems. He knew how big the problems were. And he knew that there were still no real answers. He knew how quickly people would forget, too.

But he had done more than raise money. He had given people a voice. He did and said things that many people wanted to do and say. A lot of people were angry about the African disaster because they believed that many people in power had let it happen. What is more, they were still letting it go on. Geldof knew this too, and he spoke loudly and clearly for all the people who were angry.

Bob Geldof spoke at meetings all over the world. He spoke to powerful people, and they listened. They listened because Geldof spoke for so many people. They were a little afraid of him too, because he was making them look foolish.

Geldof could hardly believe that governments were listening to him. But they were, and he used the opportunity well. He could not change the world, but he could push the world's governments a little. He did not ask them for impossible changes. He asked them to give the right kind of help and advice to the people who really needed it.

The Western governments had already given millions of dollars. They had given this aid every year. But sometimes, the money had gone to the wrong people and was spent on the wrong things. Sometimes, aid had even made things worse for people.

The West had made some terrible mistakes. Western governments had not really understood African problems. For example, women grow 80 percent of the food in Africa. Yet the West had given only 2 percent of the aid to women.

The West also sent expensive farm machines to African farmers, so fewer workers were needed. The West did not realize that poor countries need more work, not less work. They did not stop to think that people in these poor countries cannot repair these expensive machines. And they cannot afford the gasoline to keep them running, either.

African governments had made mistakes too. They had made changes without listening to their people. These

"If he had been a more sophisticated man, more conscious of the difficulties of political initiative in a complex world, Geldof might never have broken through the bureaucracies which too often ensnare international relief. But his impulsive candour, exuberance, and Irish charm saw him win every argument."
Geoffrey Wansell, in London's Sunday Telegraph

changes had turned green fields into empty deserts. Bob Geldof had seen examples of these mistakes in Africa.

But Geldof knew that he did not have the answers to Africa's problems, either. So he spoke to people who did know. He asked questions and listened to answers. He wanted answers from officials of governments all over the world, and he made the officials speak honestly.

Back to Africa

There were some people who said bad things about Bob Geldof. But the newspapers did not report them. The newspapers knew Bob Geldof, and they liked him. They said he must go on — and go back to Africa.

Geldof had problems of his own — money problems. But he, too, knew that he must go. He could not leave the work half-finished. He was lucky to have Paula. She was doing well as a writer and as a television host. She could support the family.

In Africa, Geldof's toe became infected because of an ingrown toenail. The pain was so bad that he could hardly walk. But he could not let the infection stop him. He had to see everything, and he had to help the world see it too.

Two hundred Band Aid trucks took food to starving people. Three Band Aid ships went every week from London to Africa. They carried more trucks, food, tents, and medical aid.

The European Parliament
After Sudan, Geldof went to Strasbourg, France. He was asked to speak to the European Parliament. He went but did

not write a speech. Instead, he just said what he thought. He talked about the things that had made him angry.

Geldof's words made one member of the parliament very angry. He jumped to his feet and shouted at Bob. Geldof shouted back, and the man walked out.

"The worst thing is that a lot of what the European Economic Community does is excellent," Geldof said. "You are the second biggest donor in the world. The airlift you have organized to the west of the Sudan has been an incalculable success. There's no disputing that. But the stupidity is that if you'd listened to the warnings you were given in the first place, you could have built a road for what the airlift cost. And a road would have been there next year."

Bob receives a United Nations award for his Band Aid and Live Aid work. Bob went to his home city, Dublin, to receive the award from the Irish prime minister, Dr. Garret Fitzgerald.

When Geldof finished speaking, the audience clapped loudly. They clapped because they knew he was right. He was saying things that they wanted to say but couldn't. They were pleased that someone had the courage to say it.

Geldof went to Australia. He asked the Australian government to send more food to Africa. He also asked them for planes. And he asked them to help African farmers. He knew the Australian farmers could teach the Africans about farming on poor land. He did not get everything, but he did get some of it.

Sir Robert Geldof

Bob Geldof was given many awards for his work. They came from governments, universities, and even the United Nations. In July 1986, Queen Elizabeth II knighted him. Paula went with him to Buckingham Palace. She was very pleased and proud.

Geldof accepted the awards for all the people who had helped him: his friends, the organizers of Band Aid, the pop stars, and above all, Paula.

People from all over the world were still giving money. The Live Aid concert was soon followed by Actor Aid, Art Aid, Fashion Aid, School Aid, Sports Aid, and many other aid campaigns in many different countries.

Some of the money bought things that were needed immediately: food, trucks and ships, clothes and medicine. These things saved people on the edge of death. But Band Aid also gave people the chance to begin life again. It built houses, schools, and clinics. It helped small farmers rebuild after the famine, giving them new supplies and new animals. In Ethiopia, Sudan, Mali, and Chad, money went to people who needed it.

Bob Geldof made the whole world aware of Africa's problems. He helped people share their pain. Changes have been made, but the problems have not gone away. People are still starving.

"We could spend our money tomorrow, and it could keep thirty million people alive for seven weeks, and then they'd die. Or, we can build wells and give them a life. I prefer to do that."

Bob Geldof

Above: Bob Geldof and the head of Band Aid, Kevin Jendon, in Addis Ababa. Between them sits a government official from Ethiopia. The board behind them shows total donations from around the world.

Opposite: Bob and all aid workers want to stop the next disaster before it happens. This mother and her child have lived through one famine. They may not live through the next one.

People are still homeless. People are still afraid. And still no one has found real answers to these problems.

An article in a London newspaper, the *Observer*, stated the facts: "Incomes are now lower than they were in 1970, and are expected to fall . . . for the next decade. A fifth less food is produced for every African than in 1960; if this trend continues, the crop in 1988 will be no better than 1984's disastrous harvest, even if the rains are good.

"Much of this," the article added, "is the fault of African governments who have starved their farmers of resources. . . . But just as much, if not more, has been beyond their control."

Bob accepts another award. This one comes from the University of Kent. The awards keep coming in for this scruffy, blunt Irishman. But it's easy to forget the rude language when a man has raised over $110 million for the world's poorest people.

Bob Geldof was born a citizen of Ireland. But he grew up to be a citizen of the world. That doesn't mean that he makes beautiful speeches with a look of love and peace on his face. He can be difficult, loud, and very impolite. As Geldof said to a *Daily Mail* reporter, "I seem rude . . . to a lot of people, but I seemed that way at eighteen."

Geldof admits he has made mistakes. His words have sometimes hurt the wrong people. But he feels that some people need to be shocked. Some people have been hiding behind smiles and polite language for so long that they forget what is real. When someone pushes truth under their noses, it is a terrible shock.

It is usually better to be polite and calm than rude and angry. But there is a danger to people being too calm, too careful, or too slow. Sometimes, nothing gets done. Occasionally a Bob Geldof is needed to shake them up — in his own case, with amazing results!

The African famine — background information

In 1984 there was famine across Africa from Mauritania in the west to
Ethiopia in the east. Why had this famine happened? One problem was
rainfall. There had not been enough rain, so crops could not grow. One
bad year would not be a big problem. There would be enough food from
the good years before. But in the 1980s there were many bad years. In the
end there was no food left.

But dry weather was not the only problem. People in Africa now live
longer than they lived before. This is because of modern medicine,
doctors, and hospitals. So there are more people than before. These extra
people need wood for fires. They cut down more trees than before. When
the trees have gone, the wind blows the dry earth away. When it rains,
the rain washes the earth away. Then the land is no good for farming.
Crops cannot grow on the land and there is no food for the extra people.

The African countries have to borrow money from rich countries and
from banks. Every year they have to pay more money back to the rich
countries. They cannot spend money on their own people because they
have to pay the rich countries. Often they cannot pay the rich countries,
so they have to borrow more money. So things get worse. And worse.

There are other problems too. In some parts of these countries there are
no roads. There have been wars in Ethiopia, Sudan, and Chad for many
years. Governments spend money on the wrong things.

Aid agencies and the Ethiopian government knew that a famine was
coming. They knew this in 1983, a year before the famine came. But the
Ethiopian government seemed to do nothing. Nobody listened to the aid
agencies, and the rich countries did nothing.

In 1984, the rains did not come.

When people started dying, the television cameras arrived. The TV
pictures shocked the world. When the world realized what was
happening, aid poured into Ethiopia. But it was too late for many people.
Thirty million people were starving and one million died.

In 1985, there was plenty of rain. Farmers could grow food again. But
there was still no answer to all the long-term problems. Another dry year
came in 1988, and famine returned. A lot of aid givers realized that their
money had not really changed anything. It had helped people to stay alive
but the problems were still there. These problems will not go away until
the rich countries change their ideas and ways. The rich countries buy

"We are the world, we are the children" blasting out at the Philadelphia concert finale. One girl dressed in her "Children to Children" T-shirt made the point that it's the children who are going to be the future of the world; it's kids caring that's going to count in the future.

many things from the poor countries, but they pay the lowest possible prices. Then the rich countries sell things to the poor countries at very high prices. So it is impossible for the poor countries to grow stronger and richer.

Aid is not used carefully enough. People are not always asked what help they need. So they get the wrong kind of help. Aid must be given to the right people too. It must be given to the small farmers. In Africa, women do 80 percent of the farming work, but only 2 percent of the aid money is given to women farmers.

Lastly, people from rich countries must tell their governments to give more aid to the poorer countries of the world. They should give more aid because the people in those countries need it. But it would also be good for the rich countries. If the poor countries were stronger and richer, they could buy more things from the rich countries. That would be good for everybody. As Bob said to the European Parliament, "You need Africa as much as they need you."

To find out more . . .

Organizations

The groups listed below provide money and services to people in need around the world. If you would like to know more about their work and how you can help, write to them at the addresses listed below. When you write, be sure to tell them exactly what you would like to know. Also include your name, address, and age.

American Friends Service Committee
Literature Resource Division
Africa Hunger and Development
1501 Cherry Street
Philadelphia, PA 19102

CARE
660 First Avenue
New York, NY 10016

Disasters Emergency Committee for Ethiopian Famine Appeal
P.O. Box 999
London EX 2R 7ET
England

Lutheran World Relief
390 Park Avenue South
New York, NY 10016

Oxfam America
115 Broadway
Boston, MA 02116

Save the Children Federation
Public Affairs
54 Wilton Road
Westport, CT 06880

United Nations Children's Fund (UNICEF)
331 East 38th Street
New York, NY 10016

World Vision
919 West Huntington Drive
Monrovia, CA 91016

Books and magazine articles

The following readings concern Africa, famine, Bob Geldof, and other performers at the Live Aid concert. To learn more about these subjects, check your local library or bookstore to see if they have these books and articles or if someone there can order them for you.

About famine —

Disaster! Famines. Fadin (Childrens Press)

Famine in Africa. Timberlake (Franklin Watts)
The Hunger Road. Fine (Macmillan)

About Ethiopia —

Ethiopia. Fadin (Childrens Press)
Ethiopia. Kleeberg (Franklin Watts)
Ethiopia. Pankhurst (Chelsea House Publications)

About performers in the Live Aid concert —

"All-Out Aid: Rock's New Spirit," *Time.* January 6, 1986. J. Cocks.
"Banding Together for Africa," *Newsweek.* July 15, 1985.
Bob Geldof: The Man Behind Live Aid. Aaseng (Lerner)
"Bob Geldof: Rock and Roll's World Diplomat," *Rolling Stone.*
    July 18-August 1, 1985.
Diana Ross: Star Supreme. Haskins (Penguin USA)
Rick Springfield. Gillianti (Silver Burdett)
"Rock Around the World," *Newsweek.* July 22, 1985. B. Barol.
"Rocking the Global Village," *Time.* July 22, 1985. J. Cocks.
Tina Turner. Koenig (Crestwood House)

List of new words

aid agencies
    Groups that raise money and distribute it to poor countries.
    Sometimes these agencies merely distribute the money.

aid officials
    People who work for aid agencies.

concert
    A performance of music on a stage.

documents
    Papers required to prove something (such as a person's identity)
    or to provide information.

donations
    Money or items such as food given to a charity or people in need.

editor
    A person who is in charge of an entire newspaper or magazine or a particular section of these publications — for example, a sports editor or book editor.

famine
    A shortage of food so great that many people have to go hungry for a long time.

Holocaust
    The mass murder of Jews just before and during World War II in European countries like Germany and Poland. When this word is spelled with a lowercase letter, as *holocaust*, it is occasionally used to refer to the mass murder of any particular group.

obnoxious
    Very unpleasant; rude.

relief
    Help for those who need it.

satellites
    Machines that go around the earth, in outer space, and that can receive and send information from and to different parts of the earth.

Important dates

1954   **October 5** — Robert Frederick Zenon Geldof is born in Dublin, Ireland.

1959   Bob's mother dies.

1971   Bob leaves school and moves to London.

1972   Bob goes to Canada and works on a newspaper.

1975   Bob returns to Ireland. The Boomtown Rats organize and play in Dublin in October.

1976   The Boomtown Rats go on a national tour and travel to Holland. Bob appears on TV.

1977   The band moves to England. They make their first album, *The Boomtown Rats*, and they have a hit single, "Looking After Number One."
Bob meets Paula Yates.

1978   The Rats have their first number-one single, "Rat Trap," and make their second album, *A Tonic for the Troops*.

1979   The Rats go on their first U.S. tour and produce their third album, *The Fine Art of Surfacing*. Their new single, "I Don't Like Mondays," remains number one for weeks.

1980   The Rats produce their fourth album, *Mondo Bongo*. They tour the United States, Europe, the Far East, and Australia.

1981   The Rats' single "Banana Republic" is in Britain's Top Ten.

1982   The Rats produce their fifth album, *Five Deep*, which sells badly. Fifi Trixiebelle is born to Bob and Paula. Bob acts in a film, *Pink Floyd — The Wall*.

1984   The Rats' sixth album, *In the Long Grass*, also sells badly. Bob acts in the film *Number One*.
October — The first TV pictures of the Ethiopian famine appear worldwide.
November — Bob organizes the Band Aid record, "Do They Know It's Christmas?" The record raises $10 million. Similar records are made in twenty other countries.

1985 Bob visits Ethiopia and Sudan in January. He starts organizing Live Aid in March.
July 13 — Live Aid concert is seen by 1.5 billion people on TV. It raises $90 million by the end of the year.
October — Bob returns to Africa.

1986 The Boomtown Rats do their last tour. Bob becomes a knight. Bob's book about his life, *Is That It?*, is a best seller.

1987 A new African famine is expected. Bob flies to Ethiopia.

1988 There is no rain in Africa. Six million people cannot feed themselves. Famine and disease return.

1990 Bob and American artists Harry Belafonte and Quincy Jones begin plans for another satellite concert.

PERFORMERS

Bryan Adams 46
Adam Ant 41
Ashford and Simpson 45
Autograph 42
Joan Baez 34, 42, 47
The Beach Boys 46
The Beatles 46
Boomtown Rats 12-14, 16-18, 20, 30, 40, 49, 55, 59
David Bowie 22, 39, 43, 47
Boy George 22, 23
Peter Briquette 12, 13
Ray Charles 30
Phil Collins 42, 47
Elvis Costello 42
Gerry Cott 12, 13
Crosby, Stills, and Nash 42
Simon Crowe 12, 13
Kiki Dee 43
Jim Diamond 24
Bo Diddley 46
Dire Straits 43
Duran Duran 22, 47
Bob Dylan 30, 47
Brian Ferry 42
Johnnie Fingers 12, 13
The Four Tops 42

Frankie Goes to Hollywood 22
Hall and Oates 47
The Hooters 42
INXS 42
Michael Jackson 30
Mick Jagger 7, 43, 44, 47
Elton John 38, 43
Howard Jones 42
Judas Priest 34
Eddie Kendricks 47
Nick Kershaw 42
B. B. King 42
Patti LaBelle 44-45, 47
Simon le Bon 22
Madonna 34, 45, 46
Brian May 46
Paul McCartney 22, 39, 46, 47
Freddie Mercury 46
Alison Moyet 47
Nightlife Thugs 14
Billy Ocean 42
Opus 42
Teddy Pendergrass 45, 46
The Pretenders 46
Queen 43, 46
REO Speedwagon 42
Keith Richard 47

Lionel Ritchie 44
Gary Roberts 12, 13
The Rolling Stones 7
Diana Ross 30
David Ruffin 47
Run-DMC 42
Sade 42
Santana 46
Paul Simon 30
Spandau Ballet 22
Rick Springfield 42
Bruce Springsteen 30, 36
Status Quo 40
Sting 20
Style Council 22, 40
Pete Townshend 47
Tina Turner 30, 44, 47
Ultravox 20
Midge Ure 20, 22, 23
U2 43
Dionne Warwick 30
The Who 7, 43
Stevie Wonder 30
Ron Wood 47
Yu Rock Mission 42

Index